THE
HEARTBEAT
AS AN
ANCIENT
INSTRUMENT

DAVID SCHLOSS

DOS MADRES
2020

DOS MADRES PRESS INC.
P.O. Box 294, Loveland, Ohio 45140
www.dosmadres.com   editor@dosmadres.com

Dos Madres is dedicated to the belief that the small press is essential to the vitality of contemporary literature as a carrier of the new voice, as well as the older, sometimes forgotten voices of the past. And in an ever more virtual world, to the creation of fine books pleasing to the eye and hand.

Dos Madres is named in honor of Vera Murphy and Libbie Hughes, the "Dos Madres" whose contributions have made this press possible.

Dos Madres Press, Inc. is an Ohio Not For Profit Corporation and a 501 (c) (3) qualified public charity. Contributions are tax deductible.

Executive Editor: Robert J. Murphy

Illustration & Book Design: Elizabeth H. Murphy
www.illusionstudios.net

Typeset in Adobe Garamond Pro & Times New Roman
ISBN 978-1-948017-95-4
Library of Congress Control Number: 2020941973

First Edition
Copyright 2020 David Schloss

Published by Dos Madres Press, Inc.

ACKNOWLEDGEMENTS

Behind the Eyes, (Dos Madres Press): "Cosmetic Surgeries,"
"Facing Faces," ""A Quiet Conscience Sleeps in Thunder'"
[as "In Consequence"], "Scenes from the Affair."

The Beloved, (Ashland Poetry Press): "The Odyssey."

Big Muddy: "After *Jules and Jim.*"

Flights: "Old Sad Song."

Fugue: "Absorbed in Therapy," "Values of Antiquity."

Group Portrait From Hell, (Carnegie Mellon University
Press): "Resurrection and the Life" [as "The Gods, 2:
Resurrection."]

Open Letters: ""A Quiet Conscience Sleeps in Thunder'"

Rick Magazine: "After *Jules and Jim.*"

Front cover: detail of "Expulsion of Adam and Eve from
Eden", Masaccio, Brancacci Chapel, Santa Maria del Car-
mine, Florence, Italy, ca. 1424-1427

TABLE OF CONTENTS

I.

FIRST COUPLE

II.

COUPLINGS

III.

UNCOUPLING

For my various Muses, over many years

I.

First Couple

Grumbling all the way into a god's tight vise,
their now-opened eyes show the love that lies
like a public secret hidden within their hands.

First Couple

We fell from innocence in nakedness together,
then tried out our own clothed versions instead.
Huddling ourselves from every falling weather,
Sin's not the measure of our meanings, we said.

We did what we could in our own fallen names,
learning to teach each other new kinds of speech,
finding the revelations in spinning weather-vanes,
reading shattered shards of stones laid out beneath.

The Heartbeat is an Ancient Instrument

"Heavy rains enfolded them, thick with revelations."

The garden, full of blossoms, blossomed under waters.
Obliged to hide, we thought the rain miraculous
as its wet magic held us deep within its mirrors.
But would this teach us how to choose, or reconsider
whatever we'd done? We asked, "Let what's between us,
please, last," for that was where we wished to live forever.

Two members of one faith in love's potential religion,
we began to brood upon our former attitudes
within our previous oblivious condition.
Our faces showed an innocence of how dreamt fears
before the facts turned out, creating new sad moods
that set one pair of lovers set apart together.

More capable of what turned us inward, alive
to new days' reckonings, we grew closer as we came
to gaps between the blacks and whites of *what* and *why*.
Yet, doing nothing much about new lusts exposed,
we would soon know, in thunderclaps, how rising waves
must end their flooding before anything would grow.

What did we see then when we stared into each others'
silent violent eyes, aware only of our own truths
that would produce fresh tears and death within us after?
Since we'd ignored the Law, we'd be sent away, however
painful that slow retreat past our fated youths
turned us in wider circles, whirling towards despair.

As we set out to find the bounds of that vast garden,
we'd have a chance at some other possible lives.
Feeling rougher then, less capable of easy pardon,
forsaken beyond knowledge of our acts, those bleaker times,
once passed, were never over. For, flooding us, soon
the roiling waters seeped into our dreams, new streams

in richer soil, thickening sounds inside which each
utterance, past gibberish, would soon enough suggest
how the golden apple of our sun, its rippling heat
surrounding us, was our god's. With pounding heartbeats,
would Love fulfill with force our inchoate request
that we should never have to leave this place, these beasts?

RESURRECTION AND THE LIFE

A constantly revivifying myth,
of Eden, for example, *versus* Life,
conversely, at the very End of Days,
cleansed our attention to driven ways:

if at first there was a lot of lying about
and dreaming of our bodies in and out
of a world composed of spun-off flesh,
ourselves, and other primal elements,

conceiving how we'd go beyond toil
to a Paradise, merging with the soil,
how feasible was it to suffer things
like helpless, unreflective suffering

before we took the next logical leap
past words, their rhythms in our sleep?
Flesh coming back to us in a new rebirth
of consciousness within the midst of earth,

we'd recreate some welcome space around
souls emerging from the common ground,
languidly filling up the void, a template,
we thought, for our silent future's fate.

'A Quiet Conscience Sleeps in Thunder'
old English saying

"It was the first bite," I said, "we've kept up
   for the sake of our short end of the stick."
Then, for long moments, we lay exhausted
   in bed, heads full of injustices, struck
   by the good a god could do, or the good
we might do without shame every night.

Before we stopped making war without stop
   in our bedclothes, minds erupting into
   the inexplicable slop of creation,
   the constant caustic calluses above
our brows seemed intaglios, indicating
some dreams of a much larger, longer life.

By dawn, all our old questions remaining
   unresolved, foreboding bodies falling
toward us as far as eyes could see, forming
   their own casual gliding from their god,
"He holds our hearts half-aloft," they complained
to no one, "and He never lets us sleep."

Purified beings, uselessly beautiful,
   with wings' intense spiritual music,
those creatures went out of their ways to say,
   "It isn't just *how* you do something, but *who*
   you do it to. When a body catches fire,
there's no sense in feeling you're the flames."

Hardened by experience then, we knew
each voice as something sent to advise us
about our own fallen qualifications
as, blue-lit, sidling in, their speech bearing
deeper strains of despair, we remembered
our own old gifts from feeling so exposed.

Since we no longer cared to carry out
such measures as those voices came to swear,
there seemed no consolation in learning
to sell our souls: the eyes for which we'd fallen
would fall for other eyes, becoming still
colder because of what we'd done before.

Formed by our old ways of being, we felt
unready to choose anything more:
the soft plush flesh cushions we'd grown into,
unlike marble, weren't chaste to our touch.
As the walls around us had never been breached
before, we'd never get past those poor shores.

These were our truths as we made our paths through
labyrinths, bearing the messages that
we'd tried, side by side, for some small miracle–
especially since we'd learned sharper ways
of seeing to the ends of our days, pinning
everything, yet nothing really, down.

Then, adding new pictures on paper to
our collections, we tried to take refuge in
teachings in accordance with new rules of
making old rules obsolete. One by one,
these bright things had less and less to do with
our extinction, so it seemed useful to find

something else to study, like leaves, flowers
in soft green envelopes, those okay bouquets;
using all the big muscle groups within
our bodies then, falling from the edges
of words into wonder, trying to compose
some new paean that might feel just right.

There would be other journeys, to confront
those whose dreams of our dreams of dreams come true
came true only in collapsed oppositions,
so cold that our neighborhood froze like dead
relations after joy– whose ends confirmed
resistance to time, as if for the last time…

For now, we'll travel on, discovering
places and things we'd thought we didn't need
to know, viewing others through dark glasses,
seeing our past lives swimming before us
as formulated as tests as great as
our forever unrequited love of selves.

GREAT CHAINS OF BEING

A bride and groom setting pictures in frames, how
could we believe in or keep faith with
our previous histories, pasts strewn like
debris in clearings where we often walked,
chattering old lyrics like hard-wired texts
timeless in the re-telling?

Between this world of things and us there lies
another, trembling with such passionate
intensity that words caught in our throats
become crowded like a murder of crows,
their harsh shrieks flying up into thin air,
an untuned piano's notes.

These days our voices share the same chorus:
blaming our fluent misanthropies on
our inheritance leaves us flickering
outside the gates where, covering ourselves
in shadows, our independence ends in
a lot of blowing leaves.

With weeds exposed at the edge of a lawn,
the signs of a few still holding fast to
the same old soil, it becomes more clear that
we've been displaced, our words coming out
like violent threats from that darkened garden,
our former quiet abode.

As the partings of our legs once seemed like
an entrance to new lives, flesh stolen from
our afterlives, we start growing colder
together past those uncontrolled desires,
their diminishing, with distress we know
lies buried deep within us.

With our prior murmuring figures from
old movies thrown onto walls, all that felt
familiar before comes to coincide
with what those dead voices seem to allude:
cheerless as a blocked gravel road giving
way behind a barricade,

the precipice beyond, the greater pain
of our wandering, becoming lost in
another country for years.

In Exile

We're romantics, sleeping around corners
from places where one word may open doors,
another may change everything. But, feeling
sick of feeling extrinsic, choking on
our old desires, what must we leave behind?
Characters have to believe in themselves:
with so many others swirling about us,
how else can we know what our lives may mean?

We're convinced that at first there's *mind*, but not
what our minds we once thought made up might be
ready to know. We excavate with cold
fingers into the sub-basements of old
palaces, beneath cracked skylights leaking
their white and wintry light; then pass out
into stubble-fields where some paintings, glazed,
tilted up to the skies, continue to glow.

With tokens good from *here* to *there*, we're slowly
becoming the world's, living just moments
away from limits of self-expressions
that, before they run out, divide minds from
perceived experience of other lives'
impermanence, a consciousness in which
our words may swell out into some new song,
claiming, "We want to go around the world."

We want to extend this vision and hope
for some deepening lines, advancing,
to carry us through. Slogging on beaches,
sands weighing heavily on our feet, we see
people huddling behind laden tables,
blowing out their country's birthday candles
like new omens: while we're facing up to
others' policies, are they right or wrong?

In time, earth's bounty can't be scrubbed of all
harsh cries, much less our own contrarieties:
our ideal's to control what enslaves us,
to secure our lives against other tribes,
to be intimidating as what we feel
is threatening, with a taut caution as
our main criterion, one that our ends
each night may only make more evident.

Those giant faces we dreamed up on billboards
seem comforting then, flat figures plastered
like posters for moments when surrounding
darkness might be brought to some light,
alternatives to news we'd bear from home,
yet showing how much hard work we still have
to do when questions of what we believe
are posed at all the local capitals.

With our plans shading into somewhere else,
now we're pedaling bicycles, rolling on
as when we were first on our own, trying
to move in beauty, but breathing the same
dirty air as everyone else breathes in,
still heavy now with bright seasonal lights,
as those old times and colors bleed into
one another, before fading away.

It takes some time to move away from
empathy: we can feel it, but don't make
much headway before we empty all that
we have left. And now, as the hours pass
over our backpacks, we're still carrying
pictures within us, covered by thoughts
of liberation from this material church:
"Keep nothing as your permanent condition."

FACING FACES

1. BEHIND THE EYES

Sometimes, if I meet someone who's taken
some path I might have chosen, bohemian
or straight, it's painful to see that person
I might have been, ways I didn't go down.

If seeing things through the lens of notions
of lost selves seems difficult for me now,
once upon a time these what-if questions
weighed like so many winters on my brow.

Then I'd feel, breathing in a thinning air,
relations I'd known, their complications,
memories of leaning over others, prayers,
holding onto some fading conversations.

I turn to face these ever-changing skies
turning from day-lit to what's still dimming
beyond once-dominant, now downcast eyes,
seeking some other, forward-facing vision.

2. REINCARNATIONS

I see in the eyes of my young daughter
the excitement and fear in new adventures,
as if, while hurrying, huddling together,
we're traveling like our great-ancestors

in railway carriages, velvety leathers
across the firmer horsehair seats in coaches,
luxuriating– such are our pleasures–
in the persistence of richer textures.

Later, perhaps we'll see, passing gardens,
heroic painted statues, pinkish roses
dusty at dusk– all our senses sharpened
by stronger scents, striking heightened poses...

3. MUSEUMS WITHOUT WALLS

When passing classic plaster statues,
I know those naked men and women
as more than mere potential tempters
of god-like powers over the human.

If presently some mock such aesthetics
as ancient textbook illustrations
made into the shapes of ideal forms
that join their skins in conversations

with held positions, their perishing
past the guises of a common wish
for such imaginary monuments
still brings deep visions of immortal flesh.

In the light of such story-telling,
this stretching of the truth to be believed,
we may live in museums without walls–
but where does this leave us, how do we leave?

4. Mid-Winter's Designs

Still slumbering within mid-winter's designs,
each day brings forth the same hard news to bear,
the colors of cold earth rising in my mind,
which no wistfulness can cancel, nor tears.

Beyond these particular perturbations,
it doesn't take many days, however swirled
with clamorings of colder incarnations,
for me to be struck by an overwhelming world:

How did anyone survive this before?
Poetry of the self's one passing voice–
remembering what once was merely yours–
when passing through the moment's the only choice.

5.   IN EARLY SPRING

I look for ways to address anew some simple tasks
towards ideal projects and the questions they pose
  beyond the inevitable civilizations' crash,
  rising into clouds of dust like puffs of smoke.

Not past or present, but the future shall be known;
  will I be free to live out memories even then?
  Extending towards infinities with every line,
  will what I save die with me, or what I spend?

  Telling of early enterprises in reverse,
for now, through composing frozen pantomimes,
  "It's a fine idea," I think, "to love one's work,"
  waking up half-content at half-past six a.m.

I don't know how I might come back, or not,
and never considered such questions very wise.
  If only I were satisfied in signing up
  for life at the bottom of pastel-colored skies...

6. Meditating on Heavens

Some try to save themselves in bodies
of water, air, all floating away
like waving white sails, surrendering
to their own oblivious endings–

while I'd meditate on the heavens,
trying to keep those great gates open
beyond the differences between
past theological opinions

of our natural capacities
for emptiness– or epiphanies–
until I can feel as capable
of tragedy, or as culpable...

7. FACING FACTS

Like many others singing the same old songs,
my sites are marked with names of things deceased,
the places I've lived conveying information:
I wouldn't be accused of living at my ease.

Others report their own unique activities,
who'd never admit to any *common* projects–
yet note this to themselves around the common
dining tables of one- or two-star restaurants.

The distinctions between those going home alone
and those who only help themselves, tucked in,
are in their desires: to learn how to thrive in air
filled with bits of soil; or with swords; or pens…

If daily fits of pain help keep good doctors close,
what I would give for some professional advice:
I yearned to reach each distant country on the map,
yet never laid a finger on them, though I tried.

8. MEDIATING ENDINGS

"Good luck," I think, forgetting all about
shouldering or unraveling my vision
of truths in the moments, the turning points
of fates, the moral crux of some religions,

to focus on a ranking and breaking of souls:
like glass crashing within my chest, the task
seems inadequate when my psyche still spills
the sharpest sets of shards into my lap.

Looking back at my historical ends,
when I speak of death, *here* is what I mean,
wanting some good accounting of myself,
like a window wiped increasingly clean.

Air here seems about to burn it's so bright
as we walk back to the town. Come down
from that great height, it's brogues we hear,
too prudent to praise the world's busy hum,
"I wouldna tairnd ta luuk," upon our return.

And what of that long trek? "Insignificant,"
we think, "if fragile people feel so fraught,"
both still morose at the failures of the love
we couldn't evoke enough of by ourselves,
now winding down like a clock losing time.

"You're not to put too hard a stare on them,"
we were warned, elbows nudging our ribs,
"nor give love to them who never ask for it;
isn't that obvious?" Snapping the portraits,
we became drowned in the moments alone.

We'll walk again to where, we won't deny,
we'd loved to drink in drinking halls, alive
with dense smoke, as the local newspapers
rattled together, in tune with narrow gauge
railway tracks, heading only to their south.

If we were to read their old timetables now,
which may be made to fit inside the crooks
of our own disestablished arms, they'd feel
as modestly un-modern; but could we find
some time for us to find such heights again?

In our good time, we'll draw upon this sun
and savor this scenic light, energized when
it shines through as a charm, a perspective
on where we're from, neither extinguished
nor distinguished there, half a world away.

Valentino's dead; but there he still lives on.
Once we realized the force of old romance,
watching these people walk the stony paths
for the better parts of hours, we'd mourned.

We couldn't shy away from antique beauty
as we compared our kinds of gods to theirs,
as other generations may have done as well
in search of something, if not quite parallel.

A small family seen as children of the cold,
leaning together alone on that hard ground,
how could we wear the costumes of others
we'd try on, when we didn't live like them?

Were there answers buried in the chambers,
the courtyards, the ancient stone structures,
those records of theirs that might record us,
finally, as some small parts of their history?

Past way-stations leading out of their cities,
those stone markers set at inexact intervals,
the small paths blossomed into diffuseness;
the further we went the longer they'd seem.

While walking through all those exemplary
patterns formed in thin air, in contradiction,
we'd said, at length, *We're not through yet–
not yet–* till all the roads and words ran out.

Like kisses falling from the skies and sown
upon our skin, snow flew in and magnified
in that countryside all our staring into what
light snow settled upon the flowing waters.

THE COLD PARADES

In Katatonia this farm isn't so much
a naming of itself as a seeming truth,
slowly mounting air like an invisible
picture only of some invisible wings.

Like others who were stranded there,
whose words blew slowly by in code
we listened to like short-wave radios,
we were of such fiction-making kind.

In the beginning, there was the wind,
with tree limbs unmoving, quite still
even as we walked on frozen ground
and winds blew fiercely in our faces.

If we saw ourselves as moving apart,
our walking generated warmth when
we talked, our words like a waterfall
among the dregs of our cold parades.

Did our lives come down to no more
than trappings against all those fears
we'd known, because we couldn't be
in the same place, same plane, twice?

Though no one ever tried to warn us,
would all those speakers ever inhabit
a construable world, each dying man
enhancing the intimations of his loss?

Ever since, when we're carried away,
will there be only the wind, or words
to come back to, in the discrepancies
between us and that world, as it was?

THE ODYSSEY

for Penelope

One day, the face that I'd been looking at
so long became abstract– and when you leaned
on one leg, balancing in bitter cold,
my kiss froze on your face. Our words fell like
wet snow, the slowly gathered syllables:
"The way we were... a long trip... settled... love..."
There was no forgiveness then, nor charity,
the unfounded goodness of the human race.

And now, in the hours remaining, I have
so little faith, air falling about me
into the commonplace: I am weary
of this long journey. So I must take up
the safekeeping, a steadfast dream of home–
and as the several constellations
fatefully turn, and will return always,
my dream soon blossoms in the universe.

Just listen: the brilliant green mosses sing
at the roots of those white trees that waited
where we stood by that coast as seasons changed.
I had meant to speak then, wanted to say,
"I'll be back," even as I left you there–
but the cold spread itself in thick white circles
of air– as the sound the sea made that day
returns to me now, so far from that shore.

I'd save that taste at any cost. In sleep,
it's strong in my mouth: for the things we think
we lost sustain themselves in faithfulness,
the full assent we'd hardly realized.
Yes, we were meant to be charged, fastened,
even as I am bound back to you now–
and though seas rise against us endlessly,
you appear before me in fresh watchfulness.

Then, when my body floats into our past,
your hands will have saved what's gone from your face:
myself, lost in your eyes, beginning again.
For you have watched– and have seen nothing else
between waking and sleep– and soon there will be
a new clearness, whole days of calm, for which
you learned how to wait, to hold the hourly air
close, as now you give yourself back to love.

As though we've never lived another life,
it seems simple now: our skins breathing oil,
our flesh no longer bruising easily–
your hair hanging heavily upon you,
your face placid beneath it. When I look,
all the years of hands longing to belong
are gone: for now I've come back– and only you,
when you see me, will know I've just arrived.

Keepsakes

In the midst of our days on earth,
we walked into the darkest forest
and found a clearing into the light,
a place two people could lie down
together with ease: that new, open
exchange of skin, of bodies giving
and taking, intently to themselves,
were our gifts of each to the other.

I knew I'd needed you, as a guide
to those pleasures, and as I might
never taste a nakedness like yours
ever again, I drank from your lips
as you drank from mine. May this
keep our surfaces and depths alive
within each of us, memories fresh
keepsakes for the rest of our lives.

II.

COUPLINGS

*Romantic partners often start
without much practice when they meet,
but soon receive their lover's art,
and then repent– and then, repeat.*

AFTER *JULES AND JIM*

1. SUMMER, 1962, BROOKLYN

M., H., and I, three friends, stayed up late
talking all night before we slipped out
to some silent streets again at dawn.

As H. and I played at 'Jules and Jim,'
M., wearing my rolled up striped trousers
and baggy sweater, was Catherine,

a *femme fatale,* thin mustache drawn on,
still beautiful dressed as a young man.
Was H jealous? Devoted to M.,

yearning for her, I shared this with him…
My father found us in the morning,
misunderstanding, disapproving

of acting out innocent fancies
conveying the trappings of romance:
running around in silly costumes,

we earnestly desired to feel doomed
under some pitiless cosmic gaze
as those three sad lovers in the film.

2. WINTER, 1966, EVANSTON

She was pregnant (not by me), M. wrote,
and so I took the very next bus
from Iowa to see her, to help–

to do what? To moon some more over
my lost chances with her in the cold?
Winter was one way of facing that truth

on the North Shore of Chicago where
I'd felt lured, at well-below zero
when I arrived at her single room.

Too soon, we left for her friends' party,
me, still wired; she, withheld all the way.
We never were alone together

at that house of the friend she'd marry,
as predicted by my cold nightmares.
After we left, took another bus,

I could only sit and watch, appalled
at her flirtations with the driver–
(another driver had 'knocked her up').

3. Autumn, 1973, Nowhere

When I first heard the terrible news,
I picked a stone from a cindered path,
like the one we'd gone down years before.

"Once, I held the smoothest one," I said,
"after awhile, I felt we were friends."
Unlike that stone, she could not be moved.

She got married, kept the child; three years
later, they moved to his family farm...
With all that past particularized,

I didn't know how much pain would flow
in any other way: first, to be
memorized; then, memorialized–

a blank surface from the start, now warmed.
Eventually, I arrived again
at her hands, come to rest before sleep–

at what we'd once been– with nothing left
between us but warmth, rising like ash
while my eyes stayed focused on the end.

VALUES OF ANTIQUITY

Like the first wild horses borne from the sea,
not knowing how someday they would be broken,
I ask her name, her date of birth, then say,
"so we can collaborate past confusion."

If my audience seems too insecure,
and proves it to me by laughing too loud,
(as if she didn't get my jokes long before
I'd beaten every line into the ground),

unlike some other artists, I'd create
some masterpiece of pent up energies
in one short space of time, to intimate
to her what she has lacked romantically.

Thinking it's more desirable to fail
to commit slow suicide successfully,
I'm brash, assuming she won't fail to fall–
but might be proven wrong, dramatically.

"Now what's the point of even going out,"
she asks, "to the heart's park?" It's flaming red,
but that's not why she'd rather row a boat
and float around a mirror-lake instead.

She knows a cock crows twice: "You're not above
twisting friendship once everything's changed."
I'll leave the party with her, my latest love,
or leave her there alone, completely estranged.

SCENES FROM THE AFFAIR

Rolling beneath an avalanche of stars,
I heard her little laugh, "No change, no fate–"
for she had sent a secret note: "Let's swim.
I'm more exciting than you think I am."

Exploring out beyond and over our heads,
the dancing boat asleep in narrow straits,
soon we were getting ready to jump ship,
then swimming off together like two fish.

*

Adrift for passing hours inside a car,
in our new scenarios, the right amount
of spirits aided making surreal scenes,
tooling along, loud music playing between.

With voices rising in high-ceilinged rooms,
we wished to make a kind of map of trips
across the continent, framing these events
with lights turned down inside our favored haunts.

*

After hours, all our differences flowered:
I saw her body as another country
with its own languages, strategies, codes–
fleshy stalks waving on the sides of roads.

In one wet dream of her, back in our room,
"Our love-bites look like strawberries," she cried,
leaping in cartwheels, as if back at school;
then, laughing in my face, called me a fool.

*

I walked hunched over, to protect my heart
from evening's daily threats when day was done–
recognizing how we'd desert our rooms
each dusk, inhabiting some deeper gloom.

One evening, I went out to walk alone
to where the rusting hulls of wave-tossed boats
floating miles above the deepest ocean floor,
as if craving touch, edged closer to the shore.

EATING TOGETHER

"I had over-prepared the event,
that much was ominous."
—Ezra Pound

Holding open a door for her, she says,
I'm acting like a man– acting like
a woman, not ready for our latest
anguished revelations. Reviewing
files about ourselves, the endings ahead
for our old grating conversations,
we take some acute routes to chase after
and make war to the scores of our youth,
when our body parts never quite cohered–
for that history's never over.

At our table, meaningless rituals
mark the fragilities of our meals,
all the essentials clashing together:
there's a dynamic play of our physiques
we invest with hours of tension after
every working day, amazing each week.
Then, what I lack in skill she makes up for
with lack of grace, which not just interferes,
but savages us, when we hear the shells
of our confident cadences crack.

And there's still a bell that's always tolling
beyond us, over the horizon,
like a language that's the only willing
tool for exegesis in our wanting,
waiting, trembling hands: we'll be drawing
some fine black lines all around ourselves,
with delineations of everything
we can't look back at, like two drive-by
politicians with patrician gestures,
but clenched fists inside of our pockets.

With all-masking fears, we needn't search far
for the most dispiriting bits of flak
from our overheated talk; however,
to give in or run by her what's just
a stallion charge that by brute force forms hope,
we create some new disorientation,
because we arrive at this state only
after experiencing what changes
our terms into some higher daring moves,
pregnant fantasies we'd always lose.

Saving us from our sad surrenders
to living with such fixed certainties
of servitude that service won't assuage,
This is my best selection, each thinks,
of my own interests, alone– the glimmers
teased out of our evenings like waters
still shimmering like the heaviest dews
as our sticky language gathers, eddies,
whirlpools as it flows on, and another
garrulous chapter comes to an end.

1.

Bad occasions render understandings:
we married young, had two children,
another generation from which sex

soon faded, collapsed back to a state
in which memory's lost to language,
a glimmering knowledge of our fate.

Without much influence, we're still
not good at these bureaucratic jobs
sullying all the surfaces of our lives,

respites coming only when taken in
completely by another lover's mouth,
like those who may later die of AIDS.

We weren't so much shallow as obtuse
about all the ways we couldn't be of use.

2.

We didn't know how much more damage
would come to us before we'd go on
working together back out of the sun.

For a first hanging offense, we were
shooting our guns off at the office,
carrying on with somebody else:

"Revenge is a cheap form of mourning,
just a little tempest in a teapot,
in a nutshell," one interpreter said–

but how quantify those being tossed
unceremoniously to the curb,
the public abettors of bad behaviors?

It goes to show the others how we blew
everything we said we were going to do.

3.

We're today's token flames, we think,
of what can't be buried when, entranced,
we remain at the conference tables,

not marching to the tops of far hills,
where we still wouldn't be able to see
how to save ourselves from deeper sleep.

You wanted things like soap from abroad,
the strong scent, the hard-milled feel of it:
"If you dismiss this loss of my respect,"

you said, "I'll lose all respect for you.
It's a lot of work just trying to drag you
in for a talk– and that does no good."

*We take all such criticisms as hard
as our own narcissistic self-regard.*

4.

It's only with bemusement or dread
that we can even look at the lists
of some upcoming public events,

all those beautiful antique tables
and chairs at the Penitent Museum
that seem to goad, just to goad us on.

Everyone says that everything there
is stunning, and everyone should know
that euphoria, hearts propped up beyond

the wonderful white powders of words
casually supplied by the shrouds
of clouds that keep passing by these days.

The only place we share, like swans,
is on the waters of our cups' bronze.

5.

We'll finally admit our wrongdoings,
like some new, more personal tattoos,
like some obvious coverings up for

our flesh's mistaken takes on the world—
but it still doesn't contain the feeling
of black sands sliding beneath our feet:

depressive and regretful, but not quite
in despair, or self-loathing, at any rate,
this is how it feels to feel like failures

when knowing how hearts can be broken
won't see us through all the years in which
our deeper expectations can never be met.

We're always bored, or bored beyond bored,
as champagne comes to a glass to be poured.

6.

We won't take any means of catharsis
home in briefcase or bag, but use some
arcane documents to tell us how to live:

undeclared, running at the wrong times,
not often missed, but well-remembered
as two confessors with little to confess,

we sit in our backyard with our goods
strewn about us as in storage, children
raised to be non-political, like us–

then call the children back in the house
with the intensity, or the purity
of those with little else left to lose.

Why do we fly into windows, refuse?
Because we do, just because we do.

OLD SAD SONG

To help support our child,
I go to work each day
with tacit understanding
of how a house may prosper–
but I'm too long away.

"Forgive my ignorance–
if I knew love," I say,
"kept notes inside my head,
we wouldn't be so lonely,
things wouldn't be this way."

You lead me back inside
to where the children play,
but I just play along,
condemned to feeling wrong,
and want to get away.

You won't accept this, though,
so in this house I hide
from picture windows now,
depicting scenes outside;
guilt makes me turn away.

ABSORBED IN THERAPY

It's all that we could do
to hold up the great weights
of our heads, subjected to
disturbing interventions:

The burdens of some hats
are more than we can bear.

We set a private record
recording our attachments,
but why was love the worst
of many stringent diets?

It seemed a good example
of the temple of the flesh.

Exposing what we'd need,
to take some firmer stand,
we understood a good deal
more than we'd believed:

We'd never know what lies
deep inside us otherwise.

Now we tell what we can,
beyond what we planned,
but will such irony suffice
when we say of our lives,

We may stay together for
an hour and feel as empty?

Cosmetic Surgeries

Since money's loosened up,
we'll loose ourselves from skin
and flesh grown soft on us,
all streaming downward then;

we'll save ourselves from lives
with volumes turned too low,
give blood as others try
to unfreeze final cold.

In operating rooms
much cooler than our sense
of reason, without return
to worldly eloquence,

our new vocation seems
a modest way to praise:
"I'm doing well, in dreams– "
"Well, I can't tell, can't say…"

With changes on the surface,
what is it that we prize?
"The flesh, above all else,"
we say, "what love requires."

We'll stay inside this place
where, lidless, tears still flow;
what's lost was born of us,
what's left is burned in both.

Showering Together

You see me jealous
of the bar of soap
that touches every
part of your body

as you bend yourself
to your audience
to show off your breasts
and I catch my breath

that soon surges past
the portal of throat,
the cave of my mouth,
and out through my teeth.

Then, turning your back,
you show me your ass,
anticipating
the downiest nest…

I love the feeling
of entering you
as you start backing
against me until

you feel all filled and
I become as thrilled
by this act with you
as we continue

to move in unison
until we seem one,
until we both come,
as our will be done.

Women Carved of Marble

When they take you over,
like sculptures you're left
wanting to touch, beyond
the mysteries they'd bare
were they your new lover,

while going up and down
the ladders of those same
singular selves, it's touch
and go, so touch will feel
at last like only your own.

As you fear their leaving
at the ends of those hours
when your time's elapsed,
they'll start ratcheting up
all their hidden meanings:

Is it worse to be the lover
or the loser of their loves?
Or, will you start to try to
find some softer mouth to
mouth resuscitation, then?

PARTS

As I was worshiping at the bottom
of the body of one certain woman,
I didn't think, as I breathed aloud
how *panties* rhymes with *entries,*
I'd get all those dirty looks instead.

"Press any key," was what she said,
eyes rather angular, Mongolian even,
particularly unsuited to an antihero
holding onto our moments of flight,
falling away in desperate flippancy.

Stopped by such fierce-looking eyes,
I could tell quite well just by looking
and said, "Are you hiding something?"
to her face where she'd hidden lovers,
impudent ones, controlled by her sex.

But this was my just due, and though
my tongue lay famished in her desert
already at those far poles of my sight,
all previous zealous efforts in flames,
at best, I wasn't too depressed, until

she added, "Don't come back!" as if
she'd celebrate the end of our games.

GIRLFRIEND

My girlfriend's not feeling the least little thing:
"You're not much of a lover, are you, my big man?"
Yet, it pleases her to consider me and sing,
"You know what it's like to come into my hands."

Though sex is still on her circadian calendar,
she thinks the fleshly world is really overworked,
while the Word lives on in nave and cupola,
like a perfect blowjob inside her holy Church.

Feeling like I'm crawling up a mountainside
with as much as I can handle's intimations,
lying in my lap, she doesn't try to hide
her thoughts about my formal limitations.

Can she go on like this, a trapped bird subsisting
on some seed and other detritus she's been thrown?
In this emptying environment, resisting
any transport, she says I've always let her down.

Then, to my general consternation, she grows,
through evolutionary communion with the wild,
no longer casual, but keeps eating and blows
up enough for two, bigger and bigger with child...

Over what floats her lust? Without makeup, instead,
with a blanket of curses attending the birth
in the maternity ward's hospital bed,
she sees the aftermath fill the crust of the earth...

Will I drive her home afterward? Still unresolved,
I feel, for now, both unabashed and unabsolved.

MUTUALLY USED

She's quite used to having rough sex,
wrists tied to a bed, eyes blindfolded
with her bandanna, while a man pulls
on her hair, controlling her head while

she deep-throats him; then he plunges
his thick penis in, pumps hard and fast
to fill her with cum up to the very brim.
She loves feeling filled, all the way up

to her stomach, with that hot throbbing.
She's very orgasmic, eyes closed, giving
herself up to pleasure in this ravishment,
screaming on a bed, thinking behind lids

just of herself while he does all the work
and the secret smile on her lips and hard
breathing increase, until she must come
over and over again, and she is released.

THE LUXURY OF SEXUAL JEALOUSY

"Yes, I've been having sex with others
every weekend for years," you said
in a dream. True, because I dreamed it,

or just a signal, warning of more
troubles in bed? Then I felt that old
lust to possess, a sick sinking sense

of being possessed by obsession
for the desired object of so many
others' attentions– making me want

all the more to be the only one
caressed, or, wanting to get out of
my body, to find the requisite

sense of self-pity, still desiring
your flesh lying open to strangers,
though I thought I really wanted you

all to myself. And when we talked
about my never giving up on
trying to return to some sprawling

country where we could be rejoined,
perverse in my passion, I couldn't help
feeling enslaved by desire and fear

of abnegation to you, who were
publicly available, but never
possessed, and yet, my only lover.

III.

Uncoupling

Neither one would speak with the bulky outrage
of the middle-aged, undersexed or undersigned,
about paying off what they'd mortgaged to time.

*"The confusions of love and lust led to some physical unions
with so many foolish mistakes that would only persist in us."*
This equation was spur and bane of my miserable social life,
for what it was worth. Could any more lasting real experience
be built upon these illusions over the years? These mysteries
remained through my days as mysteries to me: so few women
would turn me on; most never engendered love in me, or even
came close to fanciful ideals; but there were some I convinced
myself I really wanted to fuck– causing me to thrill at women
I couldn't even approve of, or lust for others I didn't even like.
Was it their personal smell that trumped everything else, colors
of eyes, a touch of soft skin, the moving shapes of curving hips?
They were markers of passion, but rarely combined with respect
and admiration, or just kindness and warmth, as stupid romantic
idealizing drove me all my days– until sex itself began to be less
automatic, more problematic, and all these difficulties increased:
I couldn't love by any act of will, and found myself, as formerly,
more and more withdrawn, more often alone. Where did I get this?
From my mother, who once loved my father, maybe continued to,
but was denied, bitter and dissatisfied all her adult life: the reason,
I learned, I'd been conceived. Yet, I lived for love, loving its short
bursts of passion, satisfaction, and more: feelings of falling in love,
willed and wished for, if so rarely available in the bodies and minds
of the various unlikely candidates who'd remain like strangers to me.
For all our intimacies, we were vessels of fixed ideas, a marriage of
incompatibles: combined, we were happy, ecstatic even, for awhile–
in between were yearning searches that kept us variously occupied,
living in fantasies and an occasional privileged thrill of satisfaction.
I'd had that, though it didn't last, time spent in frustration and despair:
a foolish animal who wanted love in an agreement with equally driven

and confused women, if the right one– *a* right one– could ever be found to share my projections. What thoughts stirred behind their faces' masks as I worshiped at altars of their sex, the source from which I'd been borne? *"The secret history of my life,"* I said, *"is of the women I've slept with in it."*

THE THREAD

"Who breaks the thread, the one
who pulls, the one who holds on?"
—James Richardson

How many times did you want us to prove
our love before we agreed to give it all up?
How could you ever be persuaded that we
were acting out two different probabilities?

It's not what's within our hands that stands
between us, unlike that soft romantic glow
at the beginning of the life I'd like to think
we'd planned to give way in time to liquid

phases polishing the air, the rearrangement
of the ranges of our planets like the hidden
sources of our own identities, as if we ever
even knew what each one's orbit would be.

Then we went out where we rarely strayed,
and stayed, so we could hold to something:
like feelings, gifts we'd wanted not to care
about, but which we wouldn't live without.

In inhibiting hours, during which we might
rediscover our limits perhaps, or some new
willingness to accept old habits, we'd keep
falling asleep, calling out together, in sleep.

I can accept our not knowing why the time,
which always changes, couldn't change us;
we had undone lists for our plans, a perfect
opportunity to return to our earlier failures.

Could this be how our voices, in an antique
uselessness, in broken bodies, might speak?
For now, we're terrified, because we know
what the uses of this language might mean.

Root Poisons

If you'll allow me to offer up what our *mise
en scene* might not, I'll wait to see what's on
offer: should either of us be allowed to fuck
with others, for example; the same as when,
hearing the words, we stop to smell a weed?

As if we'd never thrown anything to anyone
like this before, each errant throw floats up
into our two-pronged brains. But we hardly
ever went anywhere unless we went too far,
as if born to wander like two runaway stars.

Or, are we both like the clunkiest ones who
feel like some damp sands beneath our feet?
"How long ago were things still okay?" I say,
taking us back to those noncommittal rooms
where we know we won't go to bed, after all.

If it's over with, with new machineries now,
our recent reflections may be recorded soon;
but we won't learn, if it teaches us anything,
because of the weak juxtapositions between
this ersatz nonchalance and our true disdain.

Strung Beads

In your words I thought
I saw the ends of thoughts
of waxing, waning other sides
of moon faces in our future,
saying, *I want a divorce.*

Then, close-in two-shots
shot from behind a shoulder:
we're standing closely together,
leaning in, while conferring
about these new relations:

It matters less than lights
at night in closed storefront
windows, I'd say, more unsure
about our house divided, as
if we'd opened ourselves

obscenely, with no other
partner around. If you'd say,
It's raining, please don't leave,
it's like saying, *Can I finally*
trust you to stay with me

until the end? But I said,
Among those others, it feels
I'm double-parked— with only
my small comfort in missing
the mystery, commonality

of bodies like hieroglyphs.
With hearts easily deranged,
I'd first heard it as if I'd heard
strains to escape or forget it,
like the doughty or proud.

So we can move your bed,
I say, *back to the other side*
of these thicker concrete walls
of our bedroom in this story
of our lost family history—

an evening's cold libidos
seen as failure confirmed by
attachment to names or colors
of lives we can't see through,
so, nonplussed, cannot *be.*

On our new stage, neither
party feels an urgency to join
the passing parade, spirit wings
unhinged, in a searing ending
or unending laughter track.

DISILLUSIONS

In our former arena there once was a snake–
and I'd been prepared for the worst, always.
Though I meant to bring lots more to a party,
our hair's become much thinner, rather ratty.

Of my objections to the nature of our nights,
you raise new doubts about those highlights:
pertaining mainly to others as I once thought?
Figure things out, you say, *or forget about it.*

In all these new essays, both to and about us,
maybe may mean *perhaps*, but rumors of lust
in the silvery mirrors aren't spun gold; in fact,
we go downhill fast, never diamond-wrapped.

As if our passions still needed welters of pain
to ever even persist, these new interpretations
cannot free us from our old mistakes anymore;
yet, we've already dealt with all of this before.

Although I feel goaded and gutted every night,
I don't complain, but think someone else might.
I'd like to think we can take things with us now,
or afterwards, away– but we might never know.

1.

If a desire to love is what would save us when
all our rocking back and forth never explained
just what it was we were supposed to be doing,
not knowing, I thought we might understand
accepting the pains of daring but damaged plans
as we picked out our future failures together.
And yet there was laughter once, we told each other
with the high thin sounds of disappointment when
we always tried to keep trying again and again.
And if anxieties we'd provoked, took part in,
left us with our lacks intact, *"Even a weed
has a couple of good days, when it flowers,"*
we said, uncertain as our marriage vows when
we wished to be alone. Yet, since I was still
much at your disposal, *If it was easiest for
me not to leave,* I thought, *then I wouldn't.*

2.

I feel driven to do things I can't say, to drop
another breath into the spreading smog:
"It's just what we are..." Soon it's January,
and my birthday, but it doesn't create
any new implications for anyone other
than myself. Feeling orphaned since
I lost my father's 'rationalism' along
with my mother's old 'supernaturalism,'
I'd heave them both like stones over enough
distance for it to be my new kind of fashion
so far away from home. When I look back,
I feel them still, like broken angel's wings,
or an old engine's knock, the constant ache.

3.

I'm one who looks with pity on the world's
stupid blocks of ice, the many angry stones
lying on the farther sides of untried borders
of glaciers put to stress tests under pressure,
a universe where time and space make all
the changes of our masses more difficult.
Now I know we're dying, but there are still
colors, subtle and vibrant as that people
of the book in which everything good is
like a floating without wings in a never-
ending vacuum, with us resting somewhere
in between. It's miraculous that I opened
that door at all. *I wanted to hear what
they'd say today,* I say, watching a boy
coming to fill a bowl beside his house
each night, turning away, pointing up
with a different finger to the black sky
above his head– as if that little figure
was my one and only starry-eyed guide.

4.

Will this be everything there will ever
be between us, and never anything else?
It's unstable, like fire burning itself out;
or a thought-safe that our minds open
in periods of crisis; as if some flowing
water will cover up our mediocrities
and flaws, as our bodies give us more
spaces of skin to live in. With our souls
assaulted, but only on an invisible scale,
if it's no longer trustworthy, all the time
we've spent is less influential these days:
It's time for some new stab at infinity,
we think, *or to just go on living,* to be.
Just think of all the energy we may save.

5.

Do you expect me to still aspire to love?
I ask, as we fall back into old dislikes.
Personalities set, we're twins in tatters,
living simply as singular beings, yet,
in our dualities, incompletely, alone.
And since neither seems to be immune to
the telling of old tales, it may be the end
of jealousies when we let the other know
what sex we get– like necessary steps
to stop the taking of our drink or drugs.
Well, I was born, but– we might say, at last,
but no one else might be with us by then
to see our mutual moves toward recovery,
musing, *Why is no one at home with us now?*
How can we answer that difficult question?
By now, I think we really can't do any worse.

AT THE AIRPORT

Staring at the godlike screen, then watching
landings through mist, I waited long enough,
now wait awhile longer while your goods go
pushing past on the airport's baggage belt.

As if you've tried coming down too soon,
is this time we spend merely distraction
from the momentum behind past moments
of pain, if we'll both break down in the end?

What held our bodies with some living touch
was just breathing in and out, and around
what we had shared. Is it worth our skins,
our guts, to feel those old selves in ourselves?

Making our own ways around everything–
was this why you had to get so far away
to find fool's gold in mines siphoned for years
from our long lists of *what's mine, what's yours?*

Taking on endings where traps have been set
beyond our comfort levels, standing by,
now it feels nothing like love, even odd
to try to find anything left between us.

EVER AFTER

Living off the streets, at home in my bed,
I go hungry, then go look for some food
after days trying to convince myself
to give up trying to continue here.

I live modestly over the garage
like a boarder, and now may come across
as some miserable wretch in my patched
baggy cardigan and shiny chinos.

I open the door and leave it ajar
for the purposes of making things clear:
my getting out is my best remedy
when typing sounds put me back to sleep.

Do I think that some bad choices of words,
among other things, might well be called trite
because of subject matter no one else
would be foolish enough to write about?

A brush with brutal facts doesn't help much
for a climb to success, fire-licked remnants
in the shape of a red sun remaining
where I last saw it sinking through the leaves.

This is my final vote on the deceased,
a wiped-out version of a lifetime cache
of diminishing experience, a noose,
as we willed it, drawn tight around everything.

DISSOLUTIONS

1. LEAKAGES

A fearful complexity's
twisting our life to tell
of one I wouldn't think
of writing down before:
we loved a lot too soon,
yet with an easing then
toward eager possibility.

But we can't talk of why
leakages fall from a sky,
or what's going on inside
our familiar family history
when we heroize ourselves
around each Pyrrhic victory
lost within this final parting.

2. OUR CLIMATE

We who feel used to doing
exactly enough of whatever
we once felt we needed to do
in the cut grass before a gated
community are constantly busy.

Couldn't we find another useful
purpose beside chasing chimeras?
On some other nights, it was just
that we wanted to lie down inside
the higher grass inside of our sleep.

74

3. Up in the Air

Lonely in the crow's nest above
the fray, where we came to seek
out a new truth, we practice our
love of the elements flowing, new
moves flowering, hastening, gone.

We do not resist as these elements
shift, revealing some flights from
our view: to see from these reports
how we could be happy, hurrying
away by ourselves far beyond us.

4. Hotel Bedrooms

As the comet returns, with its gaze
on these two reading in two chairs,
caught in brighter moods, reaching
out to test each new reappearance
beyond amazement in a winsome
ignorance or new intelligence that
"One shouldn't always equal one,
but two should always equal two,"

the two of us, smashing weapons
on a bed, are talking to ourselves:
Some of us here are still married.
If the rest of us are never getting
married, we may still sleep alone
by ourselves in another room with
a door that maybe won't be locked.

5. MARITAL DIFFICULTIES

When a knock at our door may be
an opening, in fact, into some more
needy future, it's you who make me
see those things we love to talk about
between our sheets as bodies resisting
our lower monkey brains that wake us
up each day to face our piss and shit.

As if we wished we'd held onto each
thing we were, luscious or pale, gone
over to another side, we say, *It seems
we're setting ourselves up for failures.*

6. SEXUAL RESCUE

Then, when any old world, or word,
would seem to do, there was a sexual
rescue written again over me and you,
but an inhumane condition reached so
far back inside our two bodies besides
that old begging to be satisfied: it was

our life-story, with so much or too little
energy displayed by late mornings with
our slacker integrity; and then a woman,
who had been the glummer recipient of
my bad intentions, I left to starve alone.

7. The Name of the Song

Made to carry messages from fine lines
coming to you from a middle of a night,
you write, *I need to get away from a city
of lost personality, the same old litanies
of new austerities, the name of the song
as usual: I don't want any kind of scene.*

If you can't take it, someone else might;
yet, it's not straight, as you look straight
ahead at what you saw in her face when
you sponged around, took all the money.

8. Old Calendar

You swam like a wet dog, in a body
of water for days, facing those fears
that made her make life unendurable.
All along, she was the only one who
relentlessly questioned the photos of
atrocities you saw, and said nothing.

If you develop your own prescription
for personal prosperity, would it lead
you to walk this off around the block?
Take a chapter, any chapter and verse:
why do you do it? *The things that get
me off,* you say, *are new rejections of
your former rejections: I rip them out
and salvage these reminders each day
of all our noncommittal conversations.*

9. CODA

Hoping to save nothing less than
a lost love, signifying some new
clarity about heavenly questions
of hope created by a higher logic
than any diligently clever remark,
How may we save ourselves now
from this life of disproportionate
miscalculations, we'd asked, lips
smeared until mouths became raw.

Intellects lavished on steaming up
the lavatory windows soon became
our part in different kinds of scenes:
like that sturdy little drinking glass
forgotten by us and then left behind,
there were still the old tunes playing
from our old discarded tambourines.

ON A SPEEDING TRAIN

It's refreshing to see love stories about
an older man, an older woman; but then,
those lovers may soon begin to opt out
of situations they found themselves in.

Even as memories in space and time
of w*here* or *when,* and *how and why,*
are ugly blurs, *A Speeding Train Derails*
is found in tracks running by our eyes.

And if our lives seem upside down
with new needs for some therapy now,
such piquant looks, like a cat's smiles,
turn sun-setting sessions never redder.

Our nemesis is the taxidermist, asking,
Do you still wish for the same fate again,
if it turns you off– or does it turn you on?
I don't care to fix an old shut-down plan.

We forget what all our fusses were about,
and, if all our trying still feels too trying,
there's nothing to do but silence the heart
for nights, live and forgive maybe no one.

A LATE ANSWER

"Why are there no miracles when
gods interpenetrate our world?"
We still ask the same old questions
but have no useful solutions,
inevitably still following
how we spent our time observing
how it's not so easy to take
heavy loads off anyone's back.

Complicit, complacent, heavy,
or too heady, temporarily,
we do what we think we have to
when we hardly know what to do–
letting us know how it must be
to feel forever so gravely
impoverished, the hated name
on the tongue of our enemy.

We do not smile, but spill ideas
that we used to think of as true,
just some long-discarded theories
we've since grown accustomed to,
while, after awhile, at our limits,
blushing, anything we touch looks
beyond restoring, old and cracked;
the riddling clock no longer ticks.

The End of Fall

We walk down corridors of fallen leaves
to the dead center of a windblown field,
a few wan petals rustling at these peaks
of soon to be completely withered stems

that sink into their former selves before
these natural processes, freezing them
to nothingness; yet, flowers that remain
along the sides of rusting autumn hills,

becoming thinned-out colors, hardening
to forms no longer viable, may yield–
as white-capped gardens come to represent,
beyond receding snows, in melting spring–

some reignited radiance next year.

NOTES

Page 15: the title *Museums without Walls* is from an idea formulated by André Malroux.

Page 21, line 5, may be paraphrased as, "I wouldn't have even bothered to look back at that scenery myself."

Page 23, line 14: "ancient stone structures" are *nuraghi,* conical-shaped stone houses and fortresses from Neolithic times, still scattered by the thousands across Sardinia.

Page 33: "After *Jules and Jim "* alludes to scenes in the 1962 French film directed by Francois Truffaut and starring Jeanne Moreau.

Note: all unattributed quotations in the text are by the author.

 DAVID SCHLOSS was born in Brooklyn, New York, and educated at Columbia University, The University of Southern California School of Cinema, Brooklyn College of C.U.N.Y. (BA), and The University of Iowa Writers Workshop (MFA). At the University of Cincinnati, and then at Miami University, he taught Creative Writing, Literature and Film Studies courses, retiring as Professor of English in 2014.

He has published four full poetry collections, *The Beloved*, *Sex Lives of the Poor and Obscure*, *Group Portrait from Hell*, and *Reports from Babylon and Beyond*; plus three chapbooks, *Legends*, *Greatest Hits*, and *Behind the Eyes*, as well as scores of poems in literary journals and anthologies over the years.